MAI BHAGO

in command...

Jasprit Kaur

Art Work
Amarjit Virdi
Sonal A. Virdi

D.T.F Publishers & Distributors
117 Soho Road, Handsworth
Birmingham B21 9ST, UK
email : info@dtfbooks.com
website : www.dtfbooks.com

Art Work : Amarjeet Virdi
Sonal A. Virdi

© **Text : Jasprit Kaur**
 e-mail : jupjaapun@hotmail.com

© **D.T.F Publishers & Distributors**

First Published 2004

ISBN 1-901363-46-5

With love I dedicate this book, to all the lovely Children around the world. May Gods light shine in all your hearts and inspire your souls.

I also dedicate this book to my daughter Jupjaapun Kaur, who has inspired me to write this book. Also, to my late mother Harbhajan Kaur Sandhu, who was an extraordinary woman. Full of life and love. With a strong character and full of laughter, she was an inspiration to those who had the pleasure of meeting her.

I am truly grateful to Amarjit Virdi and Sonal A. Virdi for their art work without which this book could not have been created.

My special thanks to Sukhvir Singh Kanda for his idealistic support.

I hope you enjoy reading this book as much as I have enjoyed writing it.

Jasprit Kaur

Thoughts from the author...

Are you happy with who you are? I am proud of who I am and sincerely hope that a lot of you feel the same way about yourselves. We are lucky to be brought up within a multicultural society where we are fortunate to interact with a large variety of people who originate from diverse backgrounds and beliefs. All faiths inherently possess many stories that nurture positive attributes within our character. As such this book is a small contribution to the rich heritage we all share.

In today's modern society, there are many distractions that are designed to lead us away from the path of morality and humanity. One such example are the negative images and ideals portrayed within media and street culture that influence the youth of today. If one chooses to follow such a path, it inevitably means that they are unlikely to live up to their full potential in life.

The question arises- how can we follow a more spiritual path in this day and age? One possible answer would be to contribute to society by honest work, and to serve and help others less fortunate than ourselves. Eventually this would improve society, and thus nurture positive attributes in those around us, leading to a more truthful, and therefore more spiritual environment for our souls. Elizabeth Gozney gives the following "recipe for living";

> **Take kindly thoughts with more to spare,**
> **Add tact and patience-mix with care,**
> **A dash of faith, a hope- a smile,**
> **To make it all seem worthwhile,**
> **And weigh upon the scales of life,**
> **The joy that cancels out the strife,**
> **Resulting recipes is such-**
> **It cost so little it means so much!**

When contemplating spirituality, one may ask what God "thinks" of His creation, and what His views would be in regards to our society. Hypothetically speaking, if someday He decides to give the order to the clouds to produce no more rain, to the sun to give no more heat or light, to the rivers and oceans to dry up, to the moon to retire forever, and the world to plunge into eternal darkness. Maybe this would result in a more peaceful society ?

As human beings, it is our nature to complain and grumble when given the opportunity. We grumble about the heat when it's hot, the cold when it's winter, the rain, hard work, not enough money, the list is endless. We are never satisfied!

Yet the question remains, what have we offered to God, to whom we owe our very existence? Something, in the rush to satisfy ourselves, we do not pause to think about those we may be hurting , emotionally or otherwise. What a mess it would be if God were truly to go on strike and leave the world to perish...

Mai Bhago was a brave Sikh Warrior. She was a strong lady who lived at the time of Guru Gobind Singh Ji.

Mai Bhago was raised in a small village in a time of hatred and greed.

Do you think it would be wise to bring up a lady as a coward, whose only job was to look after the house?

No! Mai Bhago's parents had a different plan. They wanted their daughter to be able to look after herself and fight for justice as and when the time came. They believed in bravery and being proud of Sikhism.

When Mai Bhago was about twenty years old, the time did come for her to fight for what she believed in.

It was the time when 40 strong brave Sikh men were fighting alongside Guru Gobind Singh Ji against the Mughal enemy.

These 40 Sikhs saw the number and force of the enemy. They believed that they would be beaten. They begged Guru Ji to let them return home to their families...

Mai Bhago heard about the return of the 40 Sikhs, without Guru Gobind Singh Ji. She could not think why these strong men would return and leave their Guru behind, alone in a battlefield.

Nobody to help
Nobody to care

She marched up to the 40 Sikhs and in a loud strong voice she said: "I will find the Guru and fight off the enemy with him, while you stay in the village to look after your homes & children!"

The 40 Sikhs felt sorry and sad that they had left their Guru behind.

They Felt restless and ashamed of their action.

What is the point of living by not following the Guru ji's teachings. Once again they were ready to return to the Guru.

⑤

Deep in their hearts, they knew what they had to do. **"Please let us go back with you to the Guru,"** they said. **"We will fight the enemy and this time we promise we will never leave our Guru again."**

Mai Bhago got ready in her battle dress. Being tall and a build to match, her large kirpan in her right hand, bow and arrows slung on her back she looked very strong.

She was ready to meet her Guru.

      She was ready to die for her Guru.

Not looking back once, she and the 40 Sikhs rode fast over the hill and far beyond. The cloud of dust made by the horse's hooves was all that was left behind in the village.

The sudden silence in the village was only to be broken by the cry of **'Bole So Nihal',** which seemed to come from the skies above.

Who is this lady?

Who has seen this lady?
Neither you or I;
But when times are very tough,
She's always passing by.

Who has seen this lady?
Neither you or I;
When 40 Sikhs are feeling down,
She's standing tall and high.

Who has seen this lady?
Neither you or I;
She's brave, bold and beautiful,
For her Guru she's ready to die.

Who has seen this lady?
Neither you or I;
She's a saint soldier,
Her spirit is ever so high

I think we know this lady,
Both you and me;
Who else, but Mai Bhago,
A super strong lady.

Dear Children

You must learn to be brave and do good things in this world.

Carry a bit of sunshine around with you today. It doesn't cost or weigh a thing - But it is more precious than gold.

Aim High. The future is in your hands. You can make a better World.

Be Proud of who you are

The Conclusion....

The battle of Muktsar

After having left their village, Mai Bhago and the 40 Sikhs joined in the famous battle of Muktsar. Mai Bhago fought bravely and so well, she had killed many Mughal soldiers.

At the end of the battle when Guru Gobind Singh Ji was looking for survivors, Mai Bhago lying wounded greeted him.

She told Guru Ji how the forty Sikhs had given up their lives for their Guru. Guru Ji was touched by Mai Bhago's sacrifice.

After recovering, Mai Bhago remained with Guru Gobind Singh Ji until he passed away in October 1708. Mai Bhago's rifle that was used in battle can still be seen at Hazur Sahib.

Forgiveness by Guru Gobind Singh Ji click slide

Meanwhile, when the forty Sikhs had abandoned Guru Ji, they had written a statement saying that "You are not our Guru, and we are not your Sikhs". As you know when they returned to their families, their wives said that they were cowards and traitors, which made the Sikh men feel ashamed and sad. When they returned to the battlefield, they fought bravely alongside Mai Bhago, thus redeeming their honour.

After a fierce battle, most of the enemy was slain, the rest withdrew from exhaustion and lack of water. When Guru Ji looked around the battlefield to see who had assisted him, he saw the familiar faces of the forty Sikhs who had abandoned him, lying in pools of blood. Only one was conscious, his name was **Mahan Singh.** Guru Ji knelt beside the Sikh and wiped his face, with tears in his eyes Guru Ji asked, **"Whatever you wish for, I shall grant".**

11

The Sikh full of emotion and remorse said, **"Please Guru Ji forgive me and my companions for our betrayal. If it is possible, please tear up the statement that we signed and once again you will be our Guru and we yours Sikhs".** Guru Ji tore up the statement (bedaava). The forty Sikhs who lay dead on the battlefields were blessed by Guru Ji as the Chali Muktay (forty liberated ones). Sikhs remember the chali mutay in their prayers (the ardas...... panj pyaaray, char sahibzaaday, chali muktay...) Gurudwara Shaheed Ganj Sahib stands on the grounds where the battle took place.

Click slide

Notes

Storytelling can be a very enjoyable experience for young children. Especially, when the story features fun and familiar characters. Stories can also be made easy when the learning is part of a shared experience between child and the parent.

Why is reading with your child important?

Schools provide the foundation for learning, but home is where these ideas and skills can be developed, extended and consolidated.

You need to enrich the overall reading experience of children. Questioning children helps them to comprehend the story and also engages their critical and creative thinking skills. By discussing the story with your child and engaging them in some suggested activities, you will be able to develop your child into an active learner.

The following pages include activities, written in the form of worksheets. Parents and teachers are advised to use these worksheets to supplement the story-telling experience.

Reflective Thinking

A. Who was Mai Bhago? How do you think she brought up as a child? Tick the correct boxes.

Doctor	☐	Timid ☐	Proud	☐	Selfish ☐
Brave	☐	Saint ☐	Sports Personality	☐	Courageous ☐
Greedy	☐	Scared ☐	Kind & Gentle Woman	☐	
Sikh Warrior ☐		Believer ☐	Helpful	☐	

B. Use three words to describe how Mai Bhago felt when the 40 Sikhs returned without Guru Ji.

☐ ☐ ☐

C. Do you know anyone in real life like the characters in this book? How are they similar?

D. Did the story make you think about yourself and the way you act and have acted in the past? For example can you think of a situation where you showed bravery and courage?

E. Write a poem about a person that you think is inspirational. What is it about this person that inspires you?

Word Scramble

Unscramble the words and write them in the boxes.
You can refer to the story. There are clues under each word.
Can you make a word in the circles.

1. AMI GBAHO-
A famous warrior

2. MERPOSI-
To give your word to someone

3. LLEVIAG-
Smaller than a town

4. YEENM-
Opposite of a friend

5. CRIFISAEC-
Give up

6. WSRARO-
Sound like word sparrow

7. PNKRAI-
One of the 5 K's in Sikhism

8. DRSLEOI-
A person in the army

9. GHTIF-
To quarrel or argue

10. RDOWAC-
The opposite of 'brave'

Colouring Page

Word Search

Mai Bhago was a strong brave lady who fought for justice. She was a believer, she believed in herself, knowing she could stand up to anyone. Most of all she believed in God. She had found the right path to her Guru.

See if you can find the following words in the word search below:

MAI BHAGO - MUKTAY - GURU GOBIND SINGH - BRAVE -JUSTICE - SIKH - SAINT - WARRIOR - BATTLEFIELD - TRUST - KIRPAN - MUGHAL ENEMY - PROUD - STRONG - TEACHINGS - MUKTSAR

M	B	S	T	R	O	N	G	N
U	A	F	D	R	B	D	N	T
G	T	I	J	F	U	V	B	E
P	T	J	B	C	X	S	A	A
K	L	H	F	H	W	C	T	C
L	E	C	B	R	A	V	E	H
E	F	H	A	A	R	G	V	I
N	I	L	D	M	R	U	O	N
D	E	F	C	B	I	R	A	G
M	L	R	P	R	O	U	D	S
M	D	Q	A	E	R	G	Z	D
U	E	V	I	G	R	O	F	E
G	F	A	G	R	R	B	F	F
H	W	J	U	S	T	I	C	E
A	T	F	O	V	Z	N	B	J
L	I	X	N	N	L	D	E	S
E	I	S	A	Y	B	S	D	K
N	L	A	P	W	S	I	K	H
E	W	I	R	R	N	N	K	G
M	A	N	I	Y	N	G	L	W
Y	A	T	K	U	M	H	G	Q
M	U	K	T	S	A	R	I	I

Betrayal and Forgiveness

The forty Sikhs thought that they were acting for the best, when they left Guru Ji in the battlefield. However, they had betrayed their leader and best friend. Some- times we, too, let people down. Like the forty Sikhs we often feel sorry and ashamed afterwards. When we treat other people badly we let God down as well.

The good news is that, although you may do bad things, God is there to forgive you, that is if you are truly sorry for what you did.
Learn from your mistakes, and God will love you even more.

It is not easy to forgive someone when they have hurt you, but it may help if you give them a second chance. Guru Ji forgave his forty sikhs who had abandoned him. He tore up the written declaration and blessed them as the chali Muktay.

In the boxes below draw or write things that you think would make God happy.

Fill in the Blanks

Brave   Proud   Forty   Fight   Bow

Village   Die Fight   Promise   Horseback

Battle   Bravery   Sword   Arrow   Guru

Strong   Leave   Bole So Nihal   Sorry

Mai Bhago was a B...............Sikh lady. Mai Bhago's parents believed in B.............. and being P.................. of Sikhism.

When Mai Bhago heard of the return of the F .... Sikh men,. she marched up to them to tell them off. The Sikh men were S.................... and sad that they had left their G..................behind

"We will F....... the enemy and this time we P............ we will never L........... our Guru they said.

Mai Bhago got ready for B...........She had a large S............ in one hand and B........and A...............in the other. She looked very S...............

She was ready to F.................... and D.......... for her Guru.

She and the forty Sikhs got on H................. and rode fast over the hill-tops. The silence in the V.................. was broken by the cry of B....................
S.........N.......................

Glossary

Bedaava - Written statement

Bole - So - Nihal - A cry of great joy, or summons for divine aid, or a call to action

Chali Muktay - The forty liberated ones

Guru - Teacher (light that dispels all darkness)

Gurudwara - Sikh Temple (Gateway to the Guru)

Hazur Sahib - A Sikh Temple in Maharashtra (India) where Guru Gobind Singh Ji Passed away.

Kirpan - Sword (one of the five K's in Sikhism)

Mai Bhago - A female Sikh warrior

Mahan Singh - The leader of the forty Sikhs

Mughal - Muslim rulers over India

Muktsar - A place in Panjab (India). Muktsar is famous for its shrines.Its an important pilgrim centre for Sikhs.

Sikhism - A progressive religion founded over 500 year ago. Sikh means to learn (to be a student)